contents

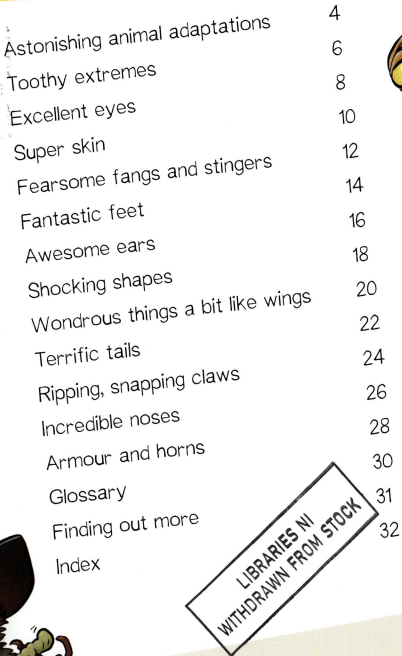

Astonishing animal adaptations

A lot of animals survive in places that would kill a human. Their bodies have evolved to suit their surroundings, however extreme. These evolutions mean some animals develop truly astonishing body bits.

A Cape ground squirrel keeps cool using its portable sunshade.

Horrendous heat

The animal world is full of clever adaptations for surviving extreme heat. They include giant ears that act as cooling towers, bushy tails that can be used as sunshades, and even tails that store fat for dry-season survival.

Chilling cold

Imagine having to walk barefoot across icy ground all day. Brr! It's no problem for the Arctic fox: it has special furry footpads on its feet to fend off frostbite.

Some tree frogs can freeze solid for weeks at a time – their hearts even stop beating – only to 'come alive' again when it warms up.

This is
the life ...

SCIENCE FLASH

'Extremophiles' are animals that can live where most species would be killed. They survive inside volcanoes and hot ocean vents, under ice, or at the bottom of the oceans.

Tardigrades (near-microscopic animals) are extremophiles. They survive being boiled, frozen, crushed and dried out. They even survive 1,000 times the radiation it takes to kill a human.

Hissss!

Fierce fighting

Horns, claws, a never-ending supply of teeth, venomous bites and stings, tails and even *heads* that can be used as clubs, poisonous skin ... animal bodies feature a LOT of parts that are perfect for fighting, whether defending, attacking or keeping their place in the pack.

Snap, snap!

Dastardly disguises

Some animals use disguises to lie in wait for prey, or to avoid being another animal's dinner. They might have bodies shaped like rocks, branches, leaves or other amazing non-animal shapes. Their skin might naturally blend in with their habitat, or it might morph in a flash to be different colours and textures at once!

5

Toothy extremes

Human teeth are all a similar shape and size (20–26 mm from root to tip). Some animals, though, have really extreme teeth.

Biggest teeth

Elephants have the biggest teeth. Their tusks are super-long teeth that grow outside of their mouths. The biggest tusks weigh over 90 kg each and are 3.4 m long. That's as heavy as a man and as long as a car.

I said NO PHOTOS!

AHH!

SCIENCE FLASH

Animal teeth are adapted to what the animal eats. Herbivores, such as giraffes, have wide, flat teeth for grinding up plants. Carnivores, such as lions, have sharp, pointed teeth for gripping and tearing meat into bits.

The biggest canines (teeth designed for biting into things like enemies and rivals) belong to hippopotamuses. Their canines can be almost a metre long. They can easily punch through the side of a tourist boat and whatever's inside!

GRIND GRIND GRIND

Yum!

Toughest teeth

The toughest teeth in the animal world belong to the limpet, a kind of seawater snail. Limpets have teeth on their tongue – about 25,000 of them! The limpet uses these mini-munchers to grind away rock. In fact, limpet teeth are the natural world's strongest material.

Replacement teeth

Humans only get one set of adult teeth. Many animals, though, are constantly growing replacement teeth. Great white sharks, for example, always have rows of new teeth forming, as replacements for old ones left behind in their prey.

Mmm ... slurp, slurp!

Teeth that don't bite

Mosquitoes have some of the smallest teeth in the animal world. They have forty-seven sharp, barb-like teeth, all so tiny that they can only be seen with a microscope. Mozzies do not use their teeth to bite, though. They use them more like saws to make way for their proboscis: a thin, sharp tube used for sucking blood.

Excellent eyes

Eagles can see about five times farther than humans.

Some animals have absolutely astounding eyes. Their eyes may be perfect for zeroing in on prey, or spotting approaching danger. Some even have eyes scattered all over their bodies ...

Eyes everywhere

One way to make sure you get a good view is to have lots of eyes. The giant clam has hundreds of pinhole eyes along its frilly mantle.

Jumping spiders have four pairs of eyes. The biggest pair face forward and focus on prey. The other pairs are angled back and are for spotting danger coming from behind.

Just TRY and surprise me.

The mantis shrimp's eyes are on stalks, and it can swivel them around separately. One eye can be looking upwards and back while the other is looking sideways.

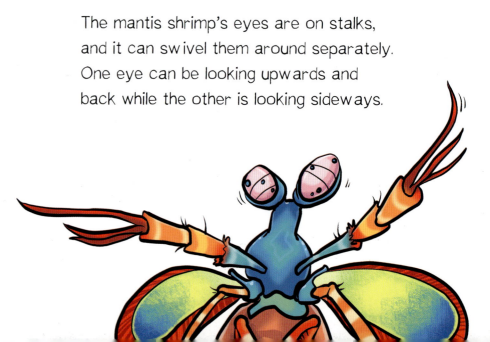

Colour at night

Most night-time hunters do not see colour well. Their eyes have lots of sensors called rods to pick up light, but few cone sensors for picking up colour.

Night-hunting geckos are different. The little lizards have no rods at all, just cones that have become super-sensitive to light. As a result, they see night-time colour three hundred times better than humans.

SCIENCE FLASH

The reason some animals – such as leopards, owls, sharks and wolves – can hunt so well in the dark, is they have a special layer called tapetum lucidum in their eyes. It reflects extra light onto their retina, making it easier to see in the dark.

Owl-o-vision

Owls are amazing night-time hunters – they can see at least ten times better in the dark than we can. Their eyes are locked forward all the time. To look from side to side they must move their head. Fortunately, owls can turn their heads through 270 degrees, so this isn't a problem.

9

Super skin

If you think skin is just something that keeps your insides in and the outside out, think again. Animal skin does some pretty sensational things.

The 'E.T.' salamander

The E.T. salamander is a freaky-looking creature from South America. The strangest thing about it, though, is how it breathes. Most amphibians breathe about 75 per cent through their lungs and 25 per cent through their skin. But E.T. doesn't have lungs. The *only* way it can breathe is by absorbing oxygen through its skin.

The 'E.T. salamander' gets its name because it looks like the film character E.T.

The thorny devil

The thorny devil lives in central Australia, where water is in short supply – so it uses its skin as a water collector. Moisture collects into drops on the lizard's strategically shaped skin, and is channelled to its mouth. If it does ever rain, the thorny devil's skin has another trick to play: water just soaks through into its body!

Not only can the thorny devil drink with its skin, it can also puff itself up to become harder for predators to swallow.

My skin's **WAY** more astounding!

No, **MINE!**

The thorny devil and E.T. salamander would never actually meet. They live on different continents!

See-through skin

Glass frogs might just have the most amazing skin of all. It's see-through, so if you look at their stomach you can see their organs working inside. They are thought to have developed see-through skin for defence. When they sit on a leaf with the light above, a predator walking below cannot see their outline. The light just shines right through!

Right! **NOW** you're in trouble!

Stretchy skin

Honey badgers have loose, stretchy skin. If something bites them, the furious honey badger twists around inside its own skin, then bites back or slashes its attacker with sharp claws.

The honey badger is not the only animal that uses stretchy skin for defence. The striped burrfish is normally only 25 cm long. When threatened, though, it puffs itself up and turns into a big, stripy ball.

Fearsome fangs and stingers

Some of the world's smallest animals are also the deadliest. That's because, though they are small, they have fangs or stingers dripping with killer **venom**.

Fangs

Venom

Vipers have long fangs, which they fold up into the roof of their mouth when not in use.

YEUW!

Venomous animals inject toxins into their victims in two main ways:

1) using fangs (long teeth with a channel or tube for injecting venom). This system is used by snakes and some spiders;

2) using stingers (hard points, sometimes with a barb attached so that it hooks into the skin as it injects the venom). Animals with stingers include wasps and some jellyfish.

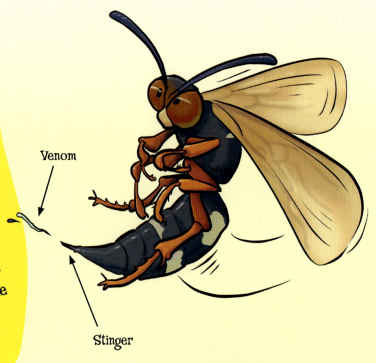

Venom

Stinger

Grumpy snakes!

Most venomous snakes only bite when they are threatened or surprised. If you back off, they do too. Australia's eastern brown snake, though, is notoriously grumpy. When disturbed, it sometimes gets so annoyed that it chases after victims, trying to bite them.

Spiders and scorpions

The Brazilian wandering spider's fangs pack what's believed to be the deadliest venom of any spider. It often goes travelling, too, hiding in cars or stowing away in bunches of bananas to visit other countries.

The deadliest of all scorpions is the fat-tailed scorpion. If you're lucky, a sting from one of these causes unconsciousness and seizures. If you're unlucky, it causes death.

Pssst! Any room for me in that bunch of bananas?

EEK!

The deadliest ... snail?

Under the sea, some cone snails hunt fish. They fire sharp, hooked fangs called radulae at passing prey. The radulae are loaded with strong venom – so strong that when humans get stung, they die unless they get medical help quickly.

Fantastic feet

You probably don't think that much about your feet (unless you've stubbed your toe). The animal world, though, has an amazing selection of jaw-dropping feet.

Camels' feet spread out and act like snowshoes to help them walk across loose sand.

Float faster, Fred! Float faster!

Slug foot

Just hanging around

The blue dragon is a kind of sea slug that hunts the deadly Portuguese man o' war. These sea slugs don't grip onto rocks, though. They grip onto the water surface from underneath, hanging around until a man o' war floats by.

Getting a grip

Flies and other insects seem to be able to walk anywhere – even upside-down on smooth glass. They can do this because of their freaky feet.

Even glass has tiny, microscopic bumps and scratches in it. The fly grips these with teeny-tiny claws at the ends of its legs. The fly's feet also have little sticky pads a bit like Velcro that give extra grip.

Teeny claw

Sticky, Velcro-like pads

Electric attraction

The hairy gecko has an extremely neat trick for running up walls. On the bottom of its feet are millions of tiny hairs. Together these produce a very small electro-magnetic force. This creates attraction between the electrons in the gecko's toes and the ones in the wall it is walking up (or down, or across).

Walking on water

Basilisks are lizards that live in Central and South America. Normally they spend their time in trees, but once in a while, a basilisk uses its hind legs to sprint across water. As its feet hit the surface, they create a tiny pocket of air underneath. The air bubble creates just enough buoyancy for one very fast step before its foot sinks.

SCIENCE FLASH

Animals weighing less than a gram can walk across water because surface tension supports their weight. Surface tension happens where a liquid touches a gas. It acts like a fragile barrier between the two fluids.

Walks on water

Awesome ears

Did you know pigeons can hear distant thunderstorms and even earthquakes coming? Here are other animals with awesome ears.

SCIENCE FLASH

Night-hunting owls have a very flat, dish-shaped face. This shape guides sounds towards the owl's ears. It can change the dish's shape using its facial muscles.

Direction finders

Barn owls can hear a mouse scratching its nose in a bush far below – then drop down silently and grab it. It's only possible because of how owl's amazing ears can detect the position of sounds:

1. Sounds of prey coming from the right reach the right ear a tiny bit quicker than the left ear.

2. The owl turns its head to the right.

3. When the sounds reach both ears at the same time, the owl knows its victim is right in front.

Cats use their ears for direction finding. They can rotate them through 180 degrees, so if they hear something interesting, turning an ear towards the sound helps them locate it.

underwater ears

Dolphins do have ears – tiny holes on the sides of their heads. But under water, dolphins don't actually bother using them. Instead they listen with their lower jaw.

Inner ear sends signals to brain

Signals pass along jaw to inner ear

Jaw

Sound waves

Hot ears

The fennec fox lives in the Sahara Desert and North Africa. The fox does not use up precious fluids by sweating out heat, as a human would. Instead, its huge ears act like blood-filled radiators, releasing heat from its body.

insect ears

When insects first emerged on Earth about 400 million years ago, they were all deaf. Most still are, but some have evolved odd hearing organs:

 • some moths, locusts and cicadas have ears in their abdomens

• crickets have an ear on each leg, just below the knee

 • mosquitoes and fruit flies have ears on their antennae

• some butterflies hear through tiny veins in their wings.

What do you mean it's hot?

17

Shocking shapes

Animals have developed an astonishing variety of shapes to help them hunt or hide.

Name: Fish-hook ant

Where: south Asia and the Pacific

Shocking shape:
a double-barbed fish hook – sharp enough to pierce skin – grows out of its back

Reason: when threatened, the ants hook themselves together and create a mass that's tricky to attack without being spiked

Name: Great orange-tip caterpillar

Where: tropical Asia

Yessssssssssss?

Shocking shape:
markings on head look like the eyes of a green vine snake

Reason: when threatened, the caterpillar lifts its head like a (venomous) vine snake about to strike. It sometimes even spits green fluid at its enemies

YEUW!

Name: Giant swallowtail caterpillar

Where: North America

Shocking shape: looks just like bird poo

Reason: to blend in while standing still, without being spotted by predators or prey

Nothing to see here. Just an innocent poo.

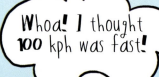

Whoa! I thought 100 kph was fast!

Name: Mata mata turtle

Where: South America

Shocking shape: the mata mata's shell, neck and head are all shaped to make it look just like a piece of bark

Reason: the mata mata's bark disguise helps it hunt and hides it from predators

Name: Tasselled anglerfish

Where: southeastern Australia

Shocking shape: the fish is disguised to look like a lump of weed-covered rock AND it has a rod with an imitation worm sticking out of its head

Reason: it lies in wait, waving its bait at passing fish. When they come close – GULP! The anglerfish swallows them down.

Speedy shapes

Some animals are specially shaped to travel at shocking speeds. On land, cheetahs can reach 100–120 kph. In the water, the black marlin can reach more than 120 kph. In the air, the free-tailed bat has recently claimed the title of fastest-known flyer, with a top speed of more than 150 kph.

Come on, you two!

Is that kitty keeping up?

wondrous things a bit like wings

Animals have developed wings for all kinds of jobs: flying long distances, hovering, acrobatics and high-speed pursuits. Most animals moving through the air are birds or insects ... but not all.

Gliding animals often have bodies with a shape that helps reduce a force called 'drag'. Drag slows down moving objects. Having a 'streamlined' shape allows the animal to glide further than it would otherwise be able to reach.

Watch out!

Sunda flying lemur

The Sunda flying lemur is not a lemur*, and it doesn't fly**. What it does do, though, is turn itself into a giant kite to move from tree to tree. Spread between its limbs is a skin membrane just 1 mm thick. Stretching this out massively multiplies the flying lemur's area and allows it to glide.

These little creatures are helpless on the ground, so they try never to touch land from birth to death.

*It's a colugo; the only other colugo species is the Philippine flying lemur (which, obviously, is also not a lemur).

**It glides.

Surprise fliers

Some surprising animals have learned how to glide or jump impressive distances:

- flying squirrels use a similar technique to colugos, and have been spotted gliding almost 50 m.

Wheeeeeee!

Yippeeee! Who needs wings?

- paradise tree snakes can jump up to 100 m from tree to tree. They flatten their body slightly and wriggle through the air at a nose-up, tail-down angle of about 25 degrees, which creates lift.

- flying fish can use their huge fins to glide up to 400 m. The fins act like glider wings, but the fish also use the updraft at the front of a wave to keep themselves in the air.

Terrific tails

Rattlesnakes shake theirs as a warning, monkeys use theirs for gripping, and male peacocks use theirs to attract a mate. But tails in the animal kingdom have an even wider set of amazing uses.

Spiny-tailed whacker

Some lizards can detach and leave their tails behind when bitten. Spiny-tailed lizards uses their tails in a more aggressive way, though: to whack their attackers. A spiny-tail usually sleeps with its tail close to the entrance of its burrow, in case it has to deter unwelcome guests.

Ocean thresher

1. Race into a school of fish

Thresher sharks have huge, whip-like tails as long as the whole rest of their body. People used to think these sharks thrashed their tails side-to-side to stun fish. We now know that what they actually do is:

2. Turn their pectoral fins and brake sharply, while also whipping their tail around over their head.

3. The whipping tail – which can reach over 120 kph – injures or destroys any fish in its path.

4. The shark has its dinner.

Tail talk

Dogs use their tails to communicate. A dog's tail might be saying the following about how it's feeling:

Held high =
'I'm the boss'

Horizontal to the ground =
'I'm exploring' (usually nose to the ground and having a good sniff, too)

Held high + fast wagging = 'I'm really happy!'

Low wagging =
'I'm a bit worried. What's going to happen?'

Tucked between legs = 'Now I'm actually scared. I give in.'

Ripping, snapping claws

Animal claws are made from keratin, the same thing as your fingernails ... but these sharp, curved rippers can be a lot more deadly than your average manicure.

Knock, knock - anyone home?

Aye-ayes love to eat insect larvae that live inside trees. The aye-aye taps with its claws and listens for movement. If it hears something, it makes a small hole in the wood. Then it reaches in with its extra-long, nail-tipped middle finger and pulls out dinner.

Digging for dinner

Armadillos use their claws to dig for their dinner. Armadillos eat all kinds of food, but their absolute favourites are ants and termites. Their long front claws rip into the hard termite mounds to get at the tasty treats inside.

Oh no! Not again!

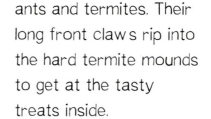

Yum! Grub!

The casso-raptor*

The cassowary (its real name) looks a bit like a giant, funky turkey, but this big bird is tough. Each powerful leg is armed with a super-long claw. It attacks like a velociraptor, kicking at its prey with its legs. Cassowaries have attacked dogs (which they really hate), cats, horses, cows – and humans.

*It's not actually called that. We made it up for fun.

Cassowaries that are used to being fed by humans sometimes attack people who don't give them food. They also attack glass doors and windows, presumably because they think they're seeing a rival cassowary.

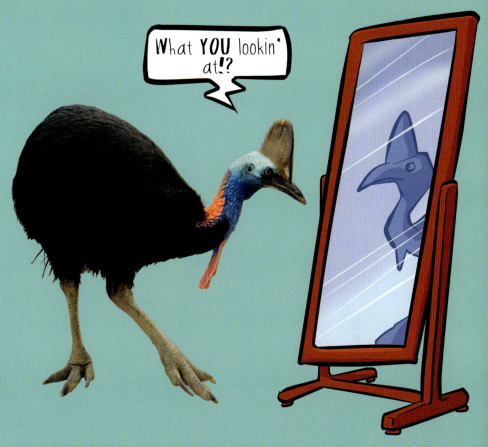

What YOU lookin' at!?

Pistol shrimp

The pistol shrimp does an amazing trick with its one giant (giant for a little shrimp, anyway) claw. The shrimp snaps the claw shut so fast that an energy pulse fires off into the water. The pulse travels at almost 100 kph, generating 218 decibels and stunning tiny fish, which the shrimp then eats.

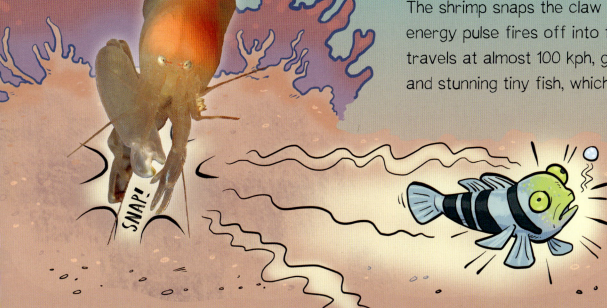

SNAP!

Incredible noses

You might think you have a good sense of smell, but you really don't. At least, not compared to elephants and some of the other super-smellers of the animal world.

How well can an elephant smell?

Some experts think elephants smell better than any other animal. They can sniff out water from almost 20 km away. African elephants can reportedly even smell the difference between tribes of people that hunt them and those that traditionally don't.

Sharks

The idea that sharks can smell just one drop of blood in the sea is wrong – but some sharks do smell food very well. The lemon shark, for example, just LOVES tuna. It could smell one drop of tuna oil in a giant swimming pool.

YEUW!

Flies love a big stink, but not just for eating. They sniff out rotting piles of rubbish for laying their eggs too. Fly mums lay their eggs inside rotting matter so the larvae can hatch and start eating and growing straight away!

DOGS

A dog's nose has about fifty times as many smell receptors as a human one. It's no wonder that bloodhounds – the dog world's best smellers – have been recorded following a scent trail that's over 300 hours old.

Nope, not dog food. But I like it.

Not mice!

Snakes

Snakes do have nostrils, but they use them more for breathing than smelling. To sniff out food, snakes use a combination of smell and taste. Snakes flick out their tongue to collect smell chemicals. They touch these to a group of sensitive cells inside their nasal passage to discover what exactly the smell is.

Armour and horns

What do your hair, a rhino's horn and a tortoise's shell have in common? They're all made of keratin. It's one of nature's toughest materials.* Keratin gets its name from the Greek work *keras*, which means 'horn'.

Go away.

Pangolin armour

A pangolin is a mammal that lives in Asia and Africa. Its skin is covered in hard scales that make up a flexible suit of armour. When threatened, the pangolin tucks in its head and curls up into a scaly ball.

Pangolin armour can't protect them against humans, though, and hundreds of thousands are killed each year for their meat and scales. Some species will soon die out completely if nothing is done to help them.

*Your hairs (and fingernails) contain a different, softer kind of keratin than the animal horns and shells.

Big-horn bashers

The biggest star of the horn-bashing world is probably the bighorn sheep. Males have huge, curled horns, which they use when fighting other males. They face each other, rear up on their back legs, and hurtle forwards at up to 30 kph. The sound of their horns crashing together can be heard kilometres away.

The bighorn's thick skull usually stops it getting too badly hurt.

Crazy big-horns

A fully grown male white rhino's horn can be 1.5 m long. In some countries the horns are mistakenly thought to have health benefits, so the rhino is a target of poachers. Sometimes live rhinos have their horns cut off to save them from these hunters.

The markhor (Asian wild goat) has amazing, twisting horns that can grow longer than the height of the average human 10-year-old!

A chameleon with horns? Yes, really. The males use them like bighorn sheep, to fight other males.

Glossary

abdomen rear part of an insect's body (which is separated into the head, thorax in the middle, and abdomen at the back)

antennae pair of long, thin stalks on the head of insects, crustaceans and some other animals, used for sensing the world around them

area amount of flat space something takes up

barb sharp point at the end of something pointy (such as a hook), which points backwards and makes the hook difficult to remove

buoyancy how well something is able to float in liquid

critically endangered soon likely to die out entirely in the wild

electron tiny particle with a negative charge, contained inside an atom

electro-magnetic combining electric currents and magnetic fields

endangered likely to die out entirely in the wild, unless action is taken

ET short for extra-terrestrial, which describes something from a planet other than Earth. ET was the name of a popular film made in 1982, featuring an ugly-but-cute alien

evolve change, over a long period of time, to be better able to live in an environment

fluid liquid or gas

habitat typical home of an animal or plant, including the other animals that live there, the landscape, plants, weather and climate

larva sometimes called caterpillars or grubs, the larva is the stage of an insect's life between egg and pupa

lichen slow-growing plant that is usually found on walls, rocks or trees

lift force that happens when a solid object and a fluid move past each other. The fluid (such as air or water) changes direction, creating lift and pushing the solid object in the opposite direction

moisture dampness in the air

organ part of a body that has its own job to do (for example, your heart is the organ responsible for pumping blood around your body)

pinhole tiny hole made by poking a pin into something, or a hole of similar size

poacher person who hunts and kills animals illegally

predator animal that hunts other animals for food

pressure force that happens when one object presses against another

radiation harmful, invisible form of energy

retina layer at back of eye that contains light-sensitive cells

toxin poison from a plant or animal

seizure sudden attack of illness, leading to loss of control of the body and sometimes jerky, twitching movements

updraft upward movement of gas against a solid object or liquid. As a wave moves forward, for example, the air in front of it is forced upwards

venom a poisin delivered by biting or stinging

vent opening that releases a fluid

vulnerable at risk of dying out entirely in the wild

wallaroo animal similar to a wallaby or kangaroo, but in between them in size

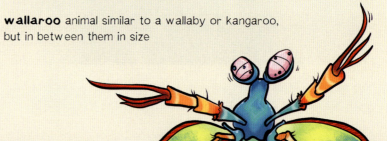

Finding out more

Books to read

If you're upset that there wasn't more about
animal poo and wee in this book, don't worry –
there are two whole books especially for you:
The Poo That Animals Do
Paul Mason and Tony de Saulles (Wayland, 2017)
The Wee That Animals Pee
Paul Mason and Tony de Saulles (Wayland, 2019)

If the facts in this book have given you an appetite for
more – things like giraffes cleaning their ears with their
tongues, or a squid's food passing through its brain before
it gets to its stomach – there are 112 pages of them in:
*50 Wacky Things Animals Do: Weird and Amazing Animal
Facts!* Tricia Martineu Wagner and Carles Ballesteros
(Walter Foster Jr, 2017)

If you'd like to know more about what goes on inside
animals, David West has written and illustrated some
beautiful short books you'll find fascinating:
Amphibians, *Birds*, *Fish*, *Mammals*, *Minibeasts* and *Reptiles*
(all published by Wayland in 2018 and 2019)

If you want to focus on some particular animal body bits,
borrow these from your local library or buy them for your
bookshelf: *Animal Tongues* and *Animal Tails*
Tim Harris (Wayland 2019)

To get to know the science behind animal and human bodies
(including tests and experiments you can do yourself):
Science Skills Sorted! Human and Animal Bodies
(Franklin Watts, 2017)

Places to visit

Great natural history museums in the UK include:
The Natural History Museum, London (nhm.ac.uk)
Great North Museum, Newcastle (twmuseums.org.uk)
The Herbert Museum, Coventry (theherbery.org)
National Museum of Scotland (nms.ac.uk)

There are lots of great zoos and safari parks you can
visit in the UK too:
ZSL London Zoo, London (zsl.org/zsl-london-zoo)
Chester Zoo, Cheshire (chesterzoo.org)
Bristol Zoo Gardens, especially the Friday Twilights
(bristolzoo.org.uk)
Belfast Zoo, County Antrim (belfastzoo.co.uk)

Get out into nature and see what amazing animals you
can spot. To find your nearest nature reserve, visit:
www.wildlifetrusts.org

Index